THE CAT'S GUIDE TO LOVE

By the same author:

Cats are Better than Men
Cats are Smarter than Men, Too!

The Cat's Guide To Love

Beverly Guhl

Hodder & Stoughton

First published in Great Britain in 1996
by Hodder & Stoughton
A division of Hodder Headline PLC

British Library Cataloguing in Publication Data
Guhl, Beverly
    The Cat's guide to love
    1. Cats – Humour 2. Cats – Caricatures and cartoons 3. American wit and humour – 20th century
    I. Title
    818.5′4′02

    ISBN 0-340-68182-9

Printed and bound in Great Britain by
Mackays of Chatham PLC, Chatham, Kent

Hodder and Stoughton
A division of Hodder Headline PLC
338 Euston Road
London NW1 3BH

The supreme happiness of
life is the conviction
that we are loved.

– Victor Hugo's cat

Beverly Guhl has designed and marketed everything from greeting cards and stationery to decorative magnets, record albums and mugs. She is the author of *Cats are Better than Men* and *Cats are Smarter than Men, Too!*. The mother of two college-age children, she lives in Texas with her husband, who she loves as much as her cat.

Part 1

LOOKING FOR LOVE

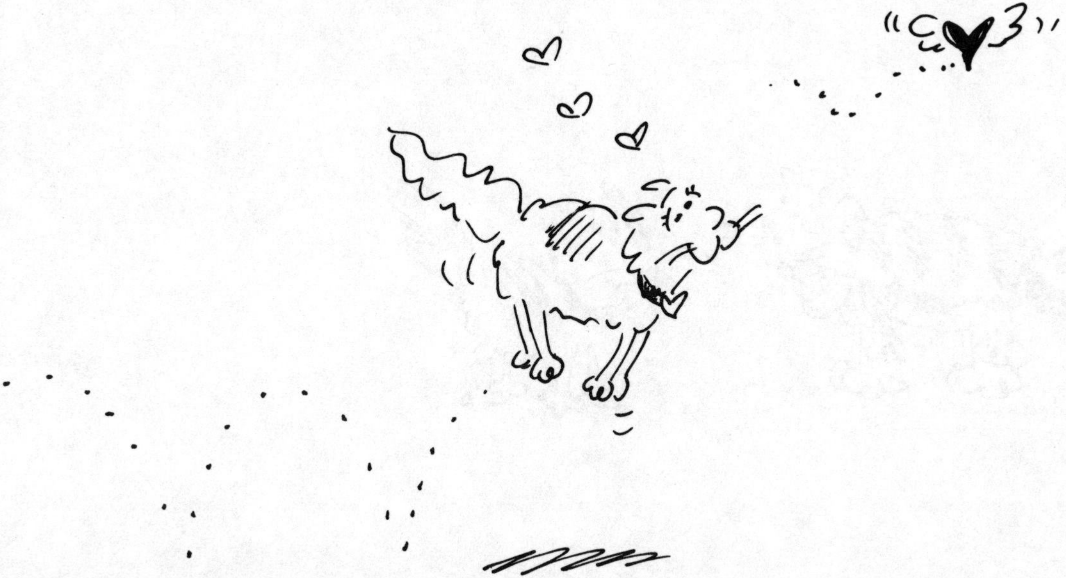

Beware of dogs in cat's clothing.

Always look your best.

A little mystery is good.

Always wear a smile.

Good pedigree is no guarantee...

for happiness.

Get plenty of beauty sleep.

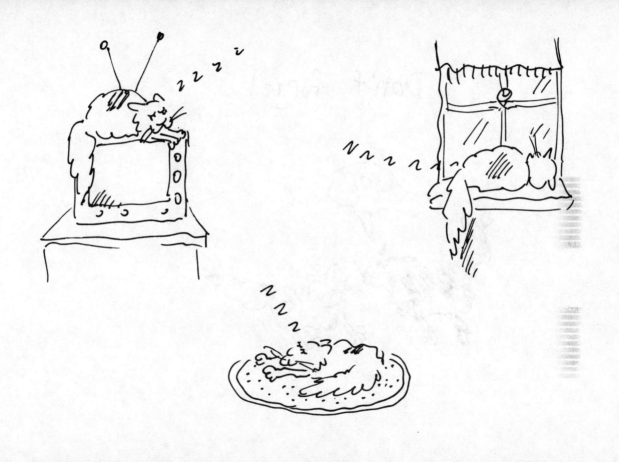

Don't forget...

It's ok to say NO.

A good book is better than...

Remember...

Sometimes Mothers DO
know best.

Part 2
FALLING IN LOVE

Know the difference between
being in **HEAT** ...

and being in *LOVE*.

Flirt
outrageously.

Be silly.

fantasize ...

daydream ...

but don't obsess.

It's ok to be aloof.

but not too aloof.

Share a romantic meal together.

Serenade each other.

Be sexy.

It's OK to walk around with
a silly smile on your face.

If you find your head is
in the clouds...

be sure your feet are
on the ground.

Have fun.

Bask in the sunshine...

play in the rain.

Exercise together.

Be helpful.

Affection is mandatory.

Explore new places together.

Meet each other's friends.

Be supportive.

Dance in the moonlight.

surprise each other
with little gifts.

Share secrets.

Plan trips together.

Communicate openly.

Take turns
chasing each other.

Be sure to
get "caught".

Explore new places to dine.

Be full of surprises.

Kiss with your
eyes open...

you'll see more.

Take time for good
grooming.

Take turns
grooming each other.

Laugh at
yourself.

Share your day.

Be a good listener.

Take naps together.

Avoid unplanned arrivals.

Know when to look the
other way...

and when NOT to.

Know when to
compromise...

and when NOT to.

Part 3

BREAKING UP

Being in LOVE...

and being in PAIN...

are not the same thing.

Know when to hold on ...

and when to let go.

You can't lose someone...

who doesn't want to get lost.

Remind yourself: if fuzzface
was so smart...

fuzzface never would have
left in the first place.

If someone doesn't love
you just the way you are...

Part 4

HEALING A BROKEN HEART

Have a good cry.

Be sure to wipe your nose.

It's ok to feel angry...

or relieved...

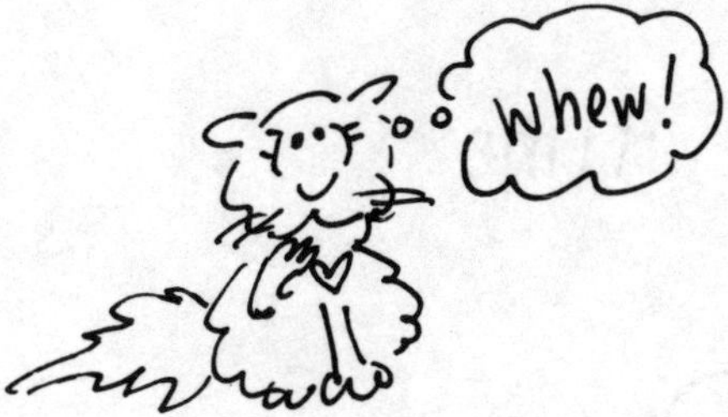

or euphoric...

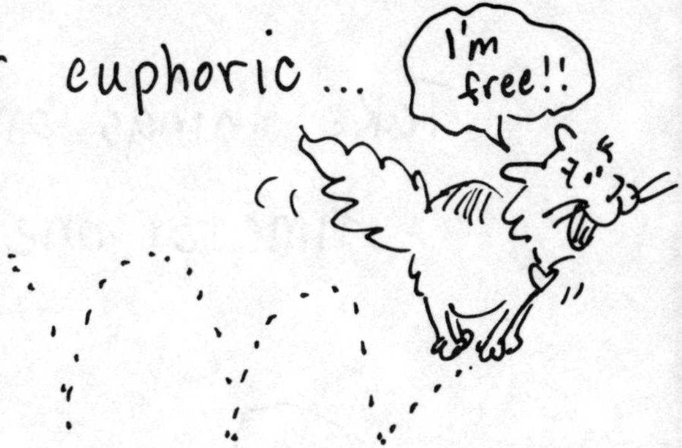

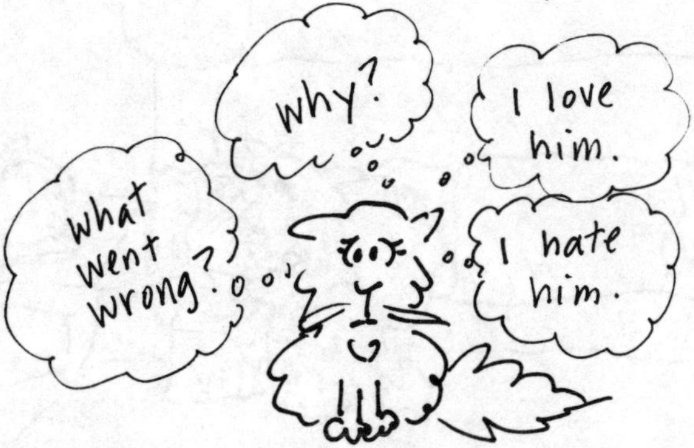

or confused, etc.

Take things one day at a
time or one hour at a time.

Love
yourself.

Pamper yourself.

Find comfort in knowing
time heals all wounds...

and wounds all heels.

Seek out sunny places
to relax.

With good friends...

who has time for
heartaches?

Put the past behind you.

Look at all the time
you have now to do
what you want to do.

Remember: there's a big difference
between being _alone_...

and being _lonely._

Daydream.

Don't rush into anything
new too soon.

Make new friends.

It's the little things
that mean a lot.

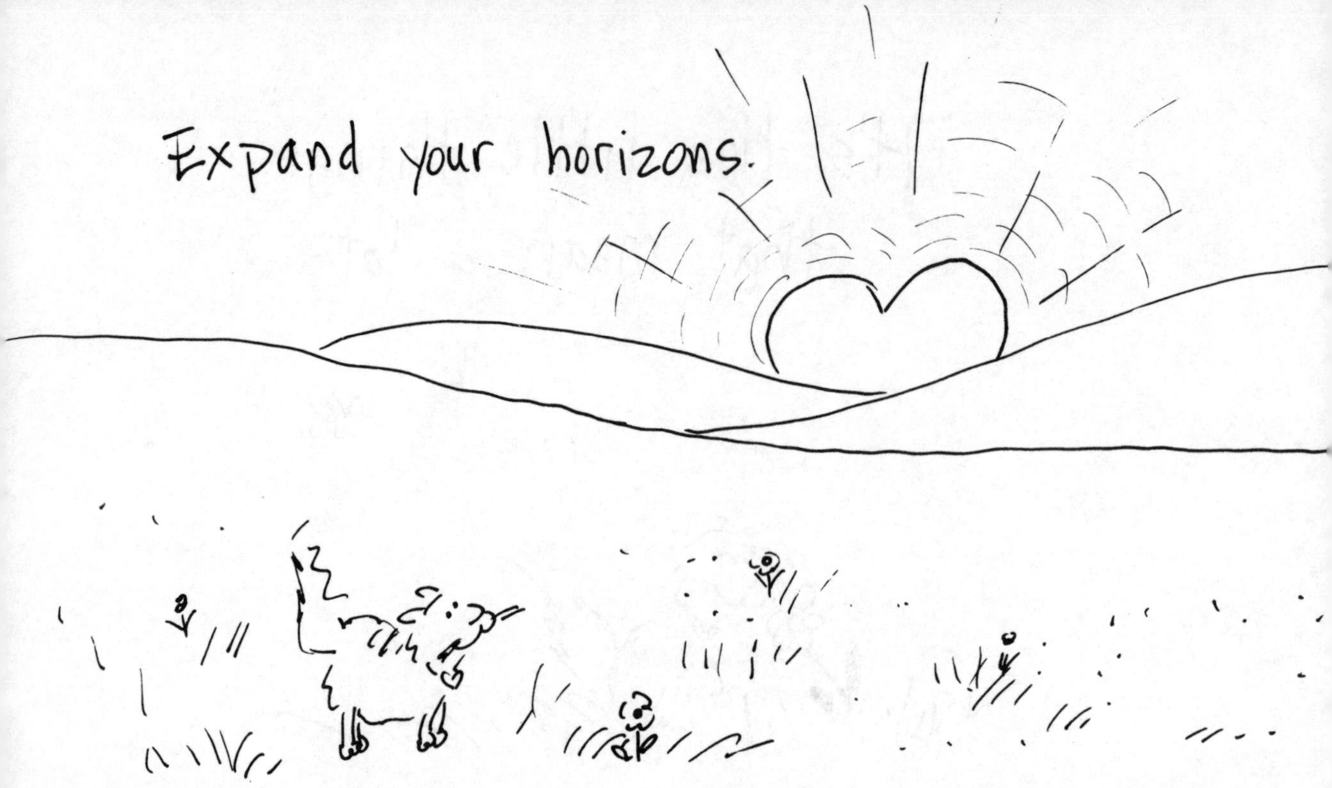
Expand your horizons.